A JOURNEY TO HEALING

A Guided Journal Through Loss, Grief, and Healing for Women

by Toshina S. Wiggins

DORRANCE PUBLISHING CO
EST. 1920
PITTSBURGH, PENNSYLVANIA 15238

Dorrance Publishing Co
585 Alpha Drive
Pittsburgh, PA 15238
Visit our website at *www.dorrancebookstore.com*

ISBN: 979-8-88729-471-1
eISBN: 979-8-88729-971-6

A JOURNEY TO HEALING

A Guided Journal Through Loss, Grief, and Healing for Women

ACKNOWLEDGMENTS

I would like to first express my deepest gratitude to God Almighty. His love lifted and sustained me during one of the most difficult and confusing seasons of my life. I am truly grateful to be used as a vessel to fulfill such an assignment to help others.

To my wonderful husband, Brandon, who is my rock and sounding board, thank you for your unconditional love and support no matter what. I love you so much!

To my amazingly brilliant son, Brayden, you are such a bright light who gives me complete joy. I am so proud to call you my son.

Lastly, this journal would not be if it were not for my little angel Brevyn, who touched my heart in such a special way. Your little footprints will remain etched in my heart forever.

DEDICATION

This journal is dedicated to all the beautiful moms who have ever experienced the loss of a child whether through miscarriage, stillbirth, and/or infant loss. There is an untapped well of strength that lies deep within you to thrive when the most unimaginable happens. You are strong! You are resilient! You are loved!

This journal belongs to:

____

MESSAGE FROM THE AUTHOR

Hello, Beautiful!

Let me first say that I am so sorry for what you are experiencing. I honor you and your loss, and you have my sincerest condolences.

Grief is extremely hard, and while everyone's journey to healing is different, I would like to encourage you to be patient and gentle with yourself while you allow yourself the space to grieve. I have learned through this process that there is no timetable to grieve and no cookie-cutter or linear path to healing; however, with time, you will find new ways to cope with your loss. I wrote the *Journey to Healing Journal* after experiencing the tremendous loss of my unborn son, Brevyn. It was written with bereaved mothers in mind but can be used by anyone who has ever experienced any loss.

I am not an expert in grief support; however, I do believe that God allowed me to go through this divine process to help others who have experienced loss, and especially those who have experienced pregnancy loss. My dear sister, I am here to tell you that you will emerge out from darkness and daybreak awaits you. Although the pain feels insurmountable, you will get through this!

As you take this journey, I pray that your heart remains open and that you find comfort and strength through writing as your heart heals. I also pray that God brings you complete and total healing: mentally, physically, emotionally, and spiritually. May His peace surround you and His powerful love draw you to healing.

The Lord is close to the brokenhearted and saves those who are crushed in spirit. The righteous person may have many troubles, but the Lord delivers him from them all. Psalm 34:18–19 **NIV**

With Love,

INTRODUCTION

Where there is Hope, there will be Healing. This was and still is my mantra as I faced the most traumatic and devastating loss of my life. There was nothing that could have prepared my husband and I for the heart-wrenching news we received on Tuesday, January 19, 2021. What started out as an exciting day turned out to be the worst day of our lives. I will never forget the words uttered by the ultrasound technician, "There is no heartbeat. I'm sorry, Mrs. Wiggins." I was nineteen weeks and three days (almost five months) pregnant. We were planning for the birth of our baby boy, not this.

So many thoughts and questions swirled around in my head as I tried to process the news. I was at a total loss. I was confused, and could not understand why something so tragic happened to me. My heart was shattered into several tiny pieces. The pain cut so deep that it felt as if it pierced the very depths of my soul. It was incomparable to anything I have ever experienced in my lifetime. My faith was challenged and world turned upside down. I was shaken to my core. I had so many questions: God, why me? How will I ever recover from this?

I have always found value in journaling, so it was only natural for me to channel my honest emotions and feelings through pen and paper. During this time, I used several different types of journals—a Gratitude Journal, Reflection Journal, Prayer Journal, and Daily Inspirational Journal. I also leaned into God's word for understanding, positioned myself in prayer, and worshipped through the pain even when I could not mutter a word and the only thing I had to offer were tears. Little did I know then that God was preparing me for this very moment. There were times when I felt so lost and alone, but God was right there all along, guiding me through this process. My journey through grief has been far from easy. The path to healing has been perfused with so many ups and downs, highs and lows, twists and turns, and more. It was during this process that I learned to be flexible and patient with myself while at the same time proclaiming my healing each and every day. I savored every joyful moment, surrendered to every painful moment, and valued the peaceful/restful moments. Ecclesiastes 7:8 declares, *Better is an end of a thing than its begin-*

ning. This promise gave me so much hope and assurance. It was through that of hope that I found solace. I anticipated my healing. It was my focal point and desired treasure. It has been and is my most prized possession.

This is my journey to healing.

ABOUT THIS JOURNAL

The *Journey to Healing Journal* is based on my personal experience with pregnancy loss and the tools I used to navigate through the grief process. This journal encompasses a compilation of healing scriptures, affirmations, quotes, and words of hope as gentle reminders to encourage one through loss and grief to a place of hope and healing. It is a guided journal that will prompt you to reflect deeply as you process your true feelings and write out your thoughts, concerns, and greatest heart's desires.

How to use your journal:

Date: _______________________________

S M T W T F S

Each day, you will have the opportunity to record the date and day of the week of each journal entry. This will allow you to revisit the entry at any point during your journey to understand what was happening at that time and also see all of the growth that is taking place.

EARLY MORNING THOUGHTS:

Journaling first thing in the morning can be really helpful to release any thoughts, emotions, feelings, or whatever comes to your mind without any judgment . It can be an opportunity for you to write during the early hours of the morning when you are having a difficult time sleeping or an opportunity to write about a dream that you had, a prayer for the day, a goal(s), or how you would like to feel by the end of the day.

____

____

____

____

3 THINGS I AM GRATEFUL FOR TODAY:

1. A good night's rest
2. Time spent with family
3. A sound mind

MY AFFIRMATION FOR TODAY:

Today, I choose to heal

What are some things you are grateful for? What positive statement(s) can you write about yourself and situation today?

There are so many great benefits to practicing gratitude and making positive declarations over your life on a daily basis. For me, the two work hand in hand with each other. Before starting your day, write out three things you are grateful for (whether big or small) and a positive affirmation about yourself, your thoughts, goals, and where you desire to be. As you do this, you are reinforcing your belief and/or desire to put you in the mindset of being where you want to be. After you write it down, say it aloud with conviction.

EVENING REFLECTIONS:

Journaling before going to bed can be really helpful to process emotions and get thoughts onto paper. Think about all aspects of your day, good or bad, and write it down. Below are some questions to ponder:

How are you feeling? What went well today? What did not go well today? Any accomplishments? What are you most proud of? What are some things you can do differently tomorrow?

QUOTE/SCRIPTURE OF THE DAY: *Each day you will find a quote or scripture at the bottom of the page to offer hope and healing. Meditate on the words written and allow them to bring comfort and peace to your heart daily.*

JOURNAL PROMPT: Journal prompts are listed each day as a statement and/or question to prompt you to write about a particular topic. They can be used as a helpful option that will assist you in getting your thoughts down on paper. Whether you choose to use the prompts is totally up to you, or you can choose to write about what you are feeling in the moment.

____

____

____

____

MY DESIRES: Towards the end of the journal, you will have an opportunity to write out your very heart's desires. Take this opportunity to focus on the positive matters of your heart. What are your desires? What are some things you would like to see happen presently and in the future? Where and how do you see yourself?

I DESIRE TO... ____

____

____

____

You will also find other guided exercises with instructions to help you express your emotions, explore your feelings, and identify your self-care needs. These practical exercises are as follows:

- Write a letter to your baby/loved one
- Write down and meditate on your favorite scripture(s)
- Practice saying aloud positive affirmations
- Practice self-care activities

At the end of this journal, you will find helpful resources that could offer support as you navigate through your loss and grief. While, I do not endorse these resources, through my personal experience and research, I have found them to be extremely beneficial while on my healing journey. I have included a few worship songs that created a comforting space for my heart to heal, books that I read to provide insightful information while moving forward and pregnancy and/or infant loss support information.

Date:

S   M   T   W   T   F   S

EARLY MORNING THOUGHTS:

3 THINGS I AM GRATEFUL FOR TODAY:

1. _______________________________
2. _______________________________
3. _______________________________

MY AFFIRMATION FOR TODAY:

EVENING REFLECTIONS:

SCRIPTURE OF THE DAY

But in my distress I cried out to the Lord; yes, I prayed to my God for help. He heard me from his sanctuary; my cry to him reached his ears. **Psalm 18:6 NLT**

JOURNAL PROMPT: *Experiencing any type of loss can be extremely overwhelming and can cause an array of emotions. How can you give yourself permission to feel the grief (i.e., anger, sadness, confusion, etc.) from your loss?*

Believe

Date: _______________

S   M   T   W   T   F   S

EARLY MORNING THOUGHTS:

____
____
____
____
____
____
____
____
____
____
____

3 THINGS I AM GRATEFUL FOR TODAY:

1. _______________________________________
2. _______________________________________
3. _______________________________________

MY AFFIRMATION FOR TODAY:

Today will be a better day

QUOTE OF THE DAY

Every journey begins with a single step – Maya Angelou

Today will be a better day

Date: ______________________

S   M   T   W   T   F   S

EARLY MORNING THOUGHTS:

____
____
____
____
____
____
____
____
____
____
____

3 THINGS I AM GRATEFUL FOR TODAY:

1. _______________________________________
2. _______________________________________
3. _______________________________________

MY AFFIRMATION FOR TODAY:

Trust the process

EVENING REFLECTIONS:

SCRIPTURE OF THE DAY

You keep track of all my sorrows. You have collected all my tears in your bottle. You have recorded each one in your book. Psalm 56:8 NLT

JOURNAL PROMPT: *God sees your pain. Even during the most difficult times, He remembers every tear we shed. Can you trust God with all of your emotions?*

Trust the process

Date: _______________

S M T W T F S

EARLY MORNING THOUGHTS:

____
____
____
____
____
____
____
____
____
____
____

3 THINGS I AM GRATEFUL FOR TODAY:

1. _______________________________________
2. _______________________________________
3. _______________________________________

MY AFFIRMATION FOR TODAY:

EVENING REFLECTIONS:

QUOTE OF THE DAY

Life isn't about waiting for the storm to pass...It's about learning to dance in the rain.
- Vivian Greene

JOURNAL PROMPT: *List at least three reasons for you to smile today...*

Faith

JOURNAL PROMPT: *List at least three reasons for you to smile today...*

Date: _______________________

S   M   T   W   T   F   S

EARLY MORNING THOUGHTS:

____
____
____
____
____
____
____
____
____
____

3 THINGS I AM GRATEFUL FOR TODAY:

1. _______________________________
2. _______________________________
3. _______________________________

MY AFFIRMATION FOR TODAY:

You are not alone

EVENING REFLECTIONS:

SCRIPTURE OF THE DAY

I will never forget this awful time, as I grieve over my loss. Yet I still dare to hope when I remember this: The faithful love of the LORD never ends! His mercies never cease. Great is his faithfulness; his mercies begin afresh each morning
- Lamentations 3:20-23 NLT

JOURNAL PROMPT: *Today, I feel … (Describe how you are feeling physically, emotionally, mentally, spiritually, etc.)*

You are not alone

Date: __________________________

S   M   T   W   T   F   S

EARLY MORNING THOUGHTS:

____
____
____
____
____
____
____
____
____
____
____
____

3 THINGS I AM GRATEFUL FOR TODAY:

1. _______________________________________
2. _______________________________________
3. _______________________________________

MY AFFIRMATION FOR TODAY:

One day at a time

QUOTE OF THE DAY

What we once enjoyed and deeply loved we can never lose, for all that we love deeply becomes a part of us. – Helen Keller

JOURNAL PROMPT: *I can remember and celebrate my baby/loved one by ...*

EARLY MORNING THOUGHTS:

3 THINGS I AM GRATEFUL FOR TODAY:

1.
2.
3.

MY AFFIRMATION FOR TODAY:

Hope

SCRIPTURE OF THE DAY

Trust in the Lord with all thine heart; And lean not unto thine own understanding. In all thy ways acknowledge him, And he shall direct thy paths. **Proverbs 3:5-6 KJV**

 In what ways can you lean into the Lord and trust Him at his word?

Hope

Breathe

EARLY MORNING THOUGHTS:

____
____
____
____
____
____
____
____
____
____
____

3 THINGS I AM GRATEFUL FOR TODAY:

1. ______________________________
2. ______________________________
3. ______________________________

MY AFFIRMATION FOR TODAY:

Breathe

QUOTE OF THE DAY

*Your hardest times often lead to the greatest moments of your life. Keep going. Tough situations build strong people in the end. – **Roy T. Bennett***

Breathe

Date: _______________________

S   M   T   W   T   F   S

EARLY MORNING THOUGHTS:

____
____
____
____
____
____
____
____
____
____
____

3 THINGS I AM GRATEFUL FOR TODAY:

1. _____________________________________
2. _____________________________________
3. _____________________________________

MY AFFIRMATION FOR TODAY:

Positive Thoughts

EVENING REFLECTIONS:

SCRIPTURE OF THE DAY

So we do not lose heart. Though our outer self is wasting away, our inner self is being renewed day by day. For this light momentary affliction is preparing for us an eternal weight of glory beyond all comparison, as we look not to the things that are seen but to the things that are unseen. For the things that are seen are transient, but the things that are unseen are eternal - II Corinthians 4:16–18 ESV

JOURNAL PROMPT: *Sometimes it is easy to lose faith in God when things do not work out how we expect them to. How can your faith carry you during this difficult time?*

Positive Thoughts

Date: _______________

S M T W T F S

EARLY MORNING THOUGHTS:

____
____
____
____
____
____
____
____
____
____
____

3 THINGS I AM GRATEFUL FOR TODAY:

1. _______________________________
2. _______________________________
3. _______________________________

MY AFFIRMATION FOR TODAY:

You are stronger than you think

QUOTE OF THE DAY

Real strength is being able to carry more than you can lift. – Brandon Wiggins

You are stronger than you think

Date: ___________________________

S   M   T   W   T   F   S

EARLY MORNING THOUGHTS:

____

____

____

____

____

____

____

____

____

____

____

____

Dream

3 THINGS I AM GRATEFUL FOR TODAY:

1. _______________________________________

2. _______________________________________

3. _______________________________________

MY AFFIRMATION FOR TODAY:

Dream

SCRIPTURE OF THE DAY

Surely he hath borne our griefs, and carried our sorrows: yet we did esteem him stricken, smitten of God, and afflicted. But he was wounded for our transgressions, he was bruised for our iniquities: the chastisement of our peace was upon him; and with his stripes we are healed - Isaiah 53:4–5 KJV

Dream

Date: _______________

S   M   T   W   T   F   S

EARLY MORNING THOUGHTS:

____
____
____
____
____
____
____
____
____
____
____

3 THINGS I AM GRATEFUL FOR TODAY:

1. _______________________________________
2. _______________________________________
3. _______________________________________

MY AFFIRMATION FOR TODAY:

Anything is possible

QUOTE OF THE DAY

Healing is embracing what is most feared, opening what has been closed, softening what has hardened into obstruction. Healing is learning to trust life. **Jeanne Achterber**

Anything is possible

Date: _______________

S   M   T   W   T   F   S

EARLY MORNING THOUGHTS:

____
____
____
____
____
____
____
____
____
____
____

Be courageous

3 THINGS I AM GRATEFUL FOR TODAY:

1. ______________________________
2. ______________________________
3. ______________________________

MY AFFIRMATION FOR TODAY:

Be courageous

SCRIPTURE OF THE DAY

I have told you these things, so that in Me you may have perfect peace. In the world you have tribulation and distress and suffering, but be courageous, be confident, be undaunted, be filled with joy; I have overcome the world. My conquest is accomplished, My victory abiding. **John 16:33 AMP**

JOURNAL PROMPT: *Listening to music can sometimes bring about a peaceful and comforting environment. Are there any particular songs that help bring comfort and healing to your heart? If so, list them here and explain how/why?*

S M T W T F S

Create

EARLY MORNING THOUGHTS:

3 THINGS I AM GRATEFUL FOR TODAY:

1.
2.
3.

MY AFFIRMATION FOR TODAY:

Create

QUOTE OF THE DAY

Healing takes courage, and we all have courage, even if we have to dig a little to find it.
- Tori Amos

JOURNAL PROMPT: *Think about the healed version of yourself. What does that look like for you? Also, describe what this experience has taught you about your own needs?*

S M T W T F S

EARLY MORNING THOUGHTS:

3 THINGS I AM GRATEFUL FOR TODAY:

1. _______________________
2. _______________________
3. _______________________

MY AFFIRMATION FOR TODAY:

Patience

SCRIPTURE OF THE DAY

For I know the plans I have for you, declares the Lord, plans to prosper you and not to harm you, plans to give you hope and a future. – Jeremiah 29:11 AMP

Patience

Date: _______________

S M T W T F S

EARLY MORNING THOUGHTS:

____
____
____
____
____
____
____
____
____
____

3 THINGS I AM GRATEFUL FOR TODAY:

1. _______________________________________
2. _______________________________________
3. _______________________________________

MY AFFIRMATION FOR TODAY:

Don't give up

QUOTE OF THE DAY

Keep your face to the sunshine and you cannot see a shadow. - Helen Keller

JOURNAL PROMPT: *In what ways can you make positivity a priority for today (thoughts, attitude, behavior, activities)?*

Date: ___________________

S   M   T   W   T   F   S

EARLY MORNING THOUGHTS:

____
____
____
____
____
____
____
____
____
____
____
____
____

3 THINGS I AM GRATEFUL FOR TODAY:

1. ______________________________
2. ______________________________
3. ______________________________

MY AFFIRMATION FOR TODAY:

This too shall pass

EVENING REFLECTIONS:

SCRIPTURE OF THE DAY

Be still, and know that I am God. Psalm 46:10 KJV

JOURNAL PROMPT: *Each day we must possess the confidence that God is God and He has everything under control. How can you remain assured of God's plan through adversity?*

This too shall pass

S   M   T   W   T   F   S

EARLY MORNING THOUGHTS:

Relax

3 THINGS I AM GRATEFUL FOR TODAY:

1.
2.
3.

MY AFFIRMATION FOR TODAY:

EVENING REFLECTIONS:

QUOTE OF THE DAY

The sun is setting on your pain and rising on your healing. – Toshina Wiggins

JOURNAL PROMPT: *Create a list of your supports. How can they help you through this healing process?*

Date: _______________________

S   M   T   W   T   F   S

EARLY MORNING THOUGHTS:

____
____
____
____
____
____
____
____
____
____
____
____

You got this

3 THINGS I AM GRATEFUL FOR TODAY:

1. _______________________________
2. _______________________________
3. _______________________________

MY AFFIRMATION FOR TODAY:

You got this

SCRIPTURE OF THE DAY

He heals the brokenhearted, and binds up their wounds (healing their pain and comforting their sorrow). **Psalm 147:3 AMP**

JOURNAL PROMPT: *None of our pain and/or trials ever catch God by surprise. What is a specific prayer you need God to answer? Journal your prayer request(s) below.*

You got this

Date: _______________

S   M   T   W   T   F   S

EARLY MORNING THOUGHTS:

3 THINGS I AM GRATEFUL FOR TODAY:

1. _______________________
2. _______________________
3. _______________________

MY AFFIRMATION FOR TODAY:

Remember to breathe

QUOTE OF THE DAY

Our wounds are often the openings into the best and most beautiful part of us.
- David Richo

JOURNAL PROMPT: *Today, I feel ...*

Date: _______________________

S   M   T   W   T   F   S

EARLY MORNING THOUGHTS:

____
____
____
____
____
____
____
____
____
____
____

3 THINGS I AM GRATEFUL FOR TODAY:

1. _______________________________
2. _______________________________
3. _______________________________

MY AFFIRMATION FOR TODAY:

EVENING REFLECTIONS:

SCRIPTURE OF THE DAY

And, he said unto me, My grace is sufficient for thee: for my strength is made perfect in weakness. Most gladly therefore will I rather glory in my infirmities, that the power of Christ may rest upon me. 2 Corinthians 12:9 KJV

Rest

Date: _______________

S M T W T F S

EARLY MORNING THOUGHTS:

____
____
____
____
____
____
____
____
____
____
____

3 THINGS I AM GRATEFUL FOR TODAY:

1. _______________________
2. _______________________
3. _______________________

MY AFFIRMATION FOR TODAY:

Joy

QUOTE OF THE DAY

All our infirmities, whatever they are, are just opportunities for God to display his gracious work in us. - C.H. Spurgeon

Joy

Date: _______________________

S   M   T   W   T   F   S

EARLY MORNING THOUGHTS:

____
____
____
____
____
____
____
____
____
____
____

3 THINGS I AM GRATEFUL FOR TODAY:

1. _______________________________
2. _______________________________
3. _______________________________

MY AFFIRMATION FOR TODAY:

Seize the day

EVENING REFLECTIONS:

____

____

____

____

____

____

____

____

____

____

____

____

____

____

____

____

____

____

SCRIPTURE OF THE DAY

And for we know that God causes everything to work together for the good of those who love God and are called according to his purpose for them. **Romans 8:28 NLT**

 Are there any goals you have accomplished recently? List them here and provide any details about how you are accomplishing your goals.

Seize the day

Date: _______________

S   M   T   W   T   F   S

EARLY MORNING THOUGHTS:

____
____
____
____
____
____
____
____
____
____
____

3 THINGS I AM GRATEFUL FOR TODAY:

1. _______________________________
2. _______________________________
3. _______________________________

MY AFFIRMATION FOR TODAY:

QUOTE OF THE DAY

I don't think of all the misery, but of all the beauty that remains. – Anne Frank

JOURNAL PROMPT: *It is easy to concentrate on the negative during adversity. What mantra can help you focus on the good during this difficult situation?*

Date: _______________________

S M T W T F S

EARLY MORNING THOUGHTS:

____
____
____
____
____
____
____
____
____
____
____
____

3 THINGS I AM GRATEFUL FOR TODAY:

1. _______________________________________
2. _______________________________________
3. _______________________________________

MY AFFIRMATION FOR TODAY:

Focus

Focus

SCRIPTURE OF THE DAY

But those who hope in the Lord will renew their strength. They will soar on wings like eagles; they will run and not grow weary; they will walk and not faint. Isaiah 40:31 NIV

JOURNAL PROMPT: *Today, I feel ...*

Date: ______________________

S M T W T F S

EARLY MORNING THOUGHTS:

____
____
____
____
____
____
____
____
____
____
____

3 THINGS I AM GRATEFUL FOR TODAY:

1. _______________________________________
2. _______________________________________
3. _______________________________________

MY AFFIRMATION FOR TODAY:

EVENING REFLECTIONS:

QUOTE OF THE DAY

Hope is like the sun, which, as we journey toward it, casts the shadow of our burden behind us. - Samuel Smiles

JOURNAL PROMPT: *What are healthy ways you can maintain balance in your life?*

Date: _______________________

S   M   T   W   T   F   S

EARLY MORNING THOUGHTS:

____
____
____
____
____
____
____
____
____
____
____
____

3 THINGS I AM GRATEFUL FOR TODAY:

1. ___________________________
2. ___________________________
3. ___________________________

MY AFFIRMATION FOR TODAY:

Stay positive

Stay positive

SCRIPTURE OF THE DAY

Count it all joy, my brothers, when you meet trials of various kinds, for you know that the testing of your faith produces steadfastness. And let steadfastness have its full effect, that you may be perfect and complete, lacking in nothing – James 1:2–4 ESV

JOURNAL PROMPT: *To have joy is a true gift from God and there is nothing anyone can do to take it away. How can you choose joy today?*

Date: _______________________

S   M   T   W   T   F   S

EARLY MORNING THOUGHTS:

____
____
____
____
____
____
____
____
____
____
____

3 THINGS I AM GRATEFUL FOR TODAY:

1. _______________________________
2. _______________________________
3. _______________________________

MY AFFIRMATION FOR TODAY:

QUOTE OF THE DAY

It is only in our darkest hours that we may discover the true strength of the brilliant light within ourselves that can never, ever, be dimmed. – Doe Zantamata

JOURNAL PROMPT: *Are you willing to embrace the mystery of God's hand working in your life even during this challenging time?*

Date:

S   M   T   W   T   F   S

EARLY MORNING THOUGHTS:

3 THINGS I AM GRATEFUL FOR TODAY:

1.
2.
3.

MY AFFIRMATION FOR TODAY:

Smile

Smile

SCRIPTURE OF THE DAY

And after you have suffered a little while, the God of all grace, who has called you to his eternal glory in Christ, will himself restore, confirm, strengthen, and establish you.
– 1 Peter 5:10 ESV

JOURNAL PROMPT: *Isn't it amazing how any kind of suffering is only temporary? Although it may not feel like it at the time, your season of darkness is not the end, but the beginning of something new. What new things are you expecting God to do in your life?*

____

____

____

____

____

____

____

____

____

____

____

____

____

____

____

____

____

____

____

____

____

____

____

Smile

Date: _______________

S   M   T   W   T   F   S

EARLY MORNING THOUGHTS:

____
____
____
____
____
____
____
____
____
____
____

3 THINGS I AM GRATEFUL FOR TODAY:

1. _____________________________
2. _____________________________
3. _____________________________

MY AFFIRMATION FOR TODAY:

Be encouraged

QUOTE OF THE DAY

It doesn't matter who you are, where you come from. The ability to triumph begins with you. – Oprah Winfrey

JOURNAL PROMPT: *Today, I feel ...*

MY DESIRES:

WRITE A LETTER TO YOUR BABY/LOVED ONE:

After about a year and three months, I was finally able to find a grief counselor who was absolutely phenomenal and who helped me tremendously during my healing journey. She provided me with the expectations of counseling from the beginning, and bottom line, I had to do the work and remain open throughout the process. This was my first time going through professional counseling. It was not easy, but one that was necessary for me to get to the next place in my journey. During our time together, she recommended an interesting exercise to complete with my husband, which was to write a letter to our sweet baby boy, Brevyn. Additionally, she suggested after we write our letters, to read them aloud to each other. During this particular assignment, we were able to express our innermost love for our baby boy in writing and the things we were looking forward to as his parents. So much healing took place just by us completing this exercise, especially in the moment of reading the letters aloud to each other.

Today, I would like to encourage you to take the opportunity to write a letter to your baby or loved one. There is something so special about getting thoughts and meaningful words about your baby/loved one down onto paper. If you have experienced pregnancy loss, stillbirth, or infant loss, write about your hopes and dreams, any thoughts or feelings about the love you share for your baby and what your little one would have brought to your family. If you experienced the loss of a loved one such as a parent, grandparent, friend, etc., reflect on the memories that you shared and how much they mean/meant to you. Write the letter as you were writing to that particular person about all the wonderful things you love(d) and how much you appreciate(d) them.

Once you have completed writing the letter, you can choose what you would like to do with it. Here are a few examples:

- Keep it private as a personal keepsake
- Seal it in an envelope and put it away in a safe place
- Read it aloud to yourself, spouse/partner, family member and/or friend

- Place it in a memorial box to read at a later time or whenever you are thinking about your baby/loved one

Other things you could do:

- Write a poem
- Write a song/rap
- Draw/Color a picture – this activity would also be great for a small child

One of my favorite scriptures is Psalm 23. I memorized it as a little girl and as I grew older, I was able to apply it to different life experiences and challenges. After my miscarriage, it became even more meaningful to me and my situation . The more I meditated on the words, the more it brought new life and strength to my heart, body, and soul.

"The Lord is my shepherd; I shall not want.
He maketh me to lie down in green pastures: he leadeth me beside the still waters.
He restoreth my soul: he leadeth me in the paths of righteousness for his name's sake.
Yea, though I walk through the valley of the shadow of death, I will fear no evil: for thou art with me; thy rod and thy staff they comfort me.
Thou preparest a table before me in the presence of mine enemies: thou anointest my head with oil; my cup runneth over.
Surely goodness and mercy shall follow me all the days of my life: and I will dwell in the house of the Lord forever."
Psalm 23 KJV

Do you have a favorite scripture that is helping you process the loss and grief of your baby/loved one? If so, write it down here and meditate on it as often as you need to.

____

____

____

____

____

____

____

____

____

____

____

____

____

ADDITIONAL SCRIPTURES FOR HOPE AND HEALING

For you created my inmost being; you knit me together in my mother's womb. I praise you because I am fearfully and wonderfully made; your works are wonderful, I know that full well. My frame was not hidden from you when I was made in the secret place, when I was woven together in the depths of the earth. Your eyes saw my unformed body; all the days ordained for me were written in your book before one of them came to be. **Psalm 139:13–16**

So do not fear, for I am with you; do not be dismayed, for I am your God. I will strengthen you and help you; I will uphold you with my righteous right hand. **Isaiah 41:10**

Cast thy burden upon the Lord, and he shall sustain thee: he shall never suffer the righteous to be moved. **Psalm 55:22**

Do not be anxious about anything, but in every situation, by prayer and petition, with thanksgiving, present your requests to God. And the peace of God, which transcends all understanding, will guard your hearts and your minds in Christ Jesus. **Philippians 4:6–7**

May the God of hope fill you with all joy and peace as you trust in him, so that you may overflow with hope by the power of the Holy Spirit. **Romans 15:13**

Yes, my soul, find rest in God; my hope comes from him. Truly he is my rock and my salvation; he is my fortress, I will not be shaken. **Psalm 62:5–6**

Being confident of this, that he who began a good work in you will carry it on to completion until the day of Christ Jesus. **Philippians 1:6**

Be strong and courageous. Do not be afraid or terrified because of them, for the Lord your God goes with you; he will never leave you nor forsake you. **Deuteronomy 31:6**

*The Lord is a stronghold for the oppressed, a stronghold in times of trouble. And those who know your name put their trust in you, for you, O Lord, have not forsaken those who seek you. **Psalm 9:9***

---

*But thou, O Lord, art a shield for me; My glory, and the lifter up of mine head. I cried unto the Lord with my voice, And he heard me out of his holy hill. I laid me down and slept; I awaked; for the Lord sustained me. **Psalm 3:3–5***

AFFIRMATIONS

I absolutely love affirmations. It is a way of training your mind to think about where you want to be and also affirming who God has already created you to be. Positive thinking was a key ingredient to my healing. On my worst days, I had to dig deep to focus on the good and approach each day with a spirit of gratitude and positivity. A great way to start getting in the habit of saying daily affirmations is by writing them down on Post-Its and sticking them to a mirror. Practice saying them in the mirror in the mornings or before going to bed.

I have included a few of my favorites for you. Remember to read them aloud with intention.

I AM GOD'S MASTERPIECE

I AM BIGGER THAN MY THOUGHTS

I AM FILLED WITH POSITIVITY

I CHOOSE JOY

I CAN BE GENTLE WITH MYSELF AS I HEAL

I CHOOSE TO FEEL AT PEACE TODAY

MY LIFE IS WHOLE AND COMPLETE

I AM GRATEFUL FOR THE LITTLE THINGS IN LIFE THAT BRING ME JOY

I BREATHE IN CALMNESS AND BREATHE OUT ANXIOUSNESS

I AM BEAUTIFUL

I AM LOVED

I AM AT PEACE

I AM HEALED

I AM WHOLE

I AM A CHILD OF THE MOST HIGH

SELF-CARE TIPS

FOCUS ON YOU!!! Being a firm believer in self-care, I have always loved pampering myself. After the miscarriage, I was more intentional about self-care than ever before. By focusing on my well-being, I was able to prioritize myself and my healing.

Although your approach to self-care may look much different from mine, it is important to take time to nurture your physical, mental, and emotional needs. God gave us only one temple to reside in and it is extremely important that we take good care of ourselves.

I did what I felt was natural to me. However, as I reflect back, I know wholeheartedly the Holy Spirit was (and still is) leading me through this process of healing.

Below, you will find a few helpful self-care tips that I explored during my journey:
- Read a new book(s)
- Join a book club
- Try a new activity
- Take a spontaneous trip
- Do something fun/exciting
- Spend time with spouse/partner
- Plan family outings
- Exercise
- Eat healthy
- Spend time in nature (walk, run, hike, go to the park)
- Start a garden
- Schedule a spa day, to include Massage Therapy, Facial, Mani/Pedi, etc.
- Explore Grief Support/Counseling
- Journal
- Read the Bible (Focus on comforting/healing scriptures)
- Meditate/Pray
- Listen to music

Think about ways you can take time for yourself and practice self-care. Write them down below.

PRAYER OF HOPE

Dear Heavenly Father, I pray for every woman that reads this journal. Give complete assurance to hope and trust in you during this difficult time. On those hard and lonely days, Father, I pray that your presence will comfort and console their hearts like no other. Thank you for granting peace that transcends all understanding and mending the pieces to broken hearts. I thank you, that there is healing after grief and your promise to give beauty for ashes is sure. Most of all, thank you for your hand being upon each and every mom and leading them to the path of divine healing. It is in your son Jesus's name, I pray. Amen!

RESOURCES

My Personal Worship Playlist

- Hallelujah – Shana Wilson
- Yahweh – Jokia
- Let Him In – Jokia
- Thy Will – Hillary Scott and the Scott Family
- The Garden – Kari Jobe
- Be Still My Soul (In You I Rest) – Kari Jobe
- Spirit Lead Me – Hillsong United
- Goodness of God – CeCe Winans
- Hymn of Breakthrough – Israel & New Breed
- Mighty One – Maverick City Music (featuring Todd Dulaney and Maryanne J. George)
- The Story I'll Tell – Maverick City Music (featuring Naomi Raine)

Helpful Books to Read

- *The Bible in 52 Weeks: A Yearlong Bible Study for Women* – by Dr. Kimberly D. Moore
- *I Know Why the Caged Bird Sings* – by Dr. Maya Angelou
- *It's Ok That You're Not Ok* – by Megan Devine
- *After the Rain* – by Alexandra Elle
- *Option B: Facing Adversity, Building Resilience, and Finding Joy* – by Sheryl Sandberg and Adam Grant
- *The Gates of Hell Shall Not Prevail: You Win* – by Apostle Matthew Tillery

Pregnancy Loss and Infant Loss Support Information

- Angel Prints Corporation – www.angelprints.org
- Share Pregnancy and Infant Loss Support – https://nationalshare.org

- March of Dimes – www.marchofdimes.org
- International Stillbirth Alliance – www.stillbirthalliance.org
- Center for Loss in Multiple Birth (CLIMB) – www.climb-support.org

National and Twenty-Four-Hour Grief Support Hotlines

- SAMHSA'S National Helpline – 1-800-662-HELP (4357)
- National Suicide Prevention Lifeline/National Crisis Hotline – 1-800-273-8255
- Crisis Text Line – Text HOME to 741-741 in the U.S.

NOTES

NOTES

NOTES